DIY Dried Flower Ideas

Making Unique and Beautiful Dried Flowers

Copyright © 2023

DEDICATION

Contents

How to Dry Flowers

If you want to know what method was used to dry the daisies in the image above, just jump down to the silica sand method. It created paperlike perfect dried flowers that kept the vibrancy of the flowers we tested.

DRYING AND PRESERVING FLOWERS – THE BEST (AND NOT SO BEST) METHODS

It's nice to save a few, preserve them and keep a bit of that summer colour living through the fall and winter.

Dried flowers are also great craft items and buying them already dried is a bit too rich for your pocketbook, so make your own.

HOW TO DRY FLOWERS WITH A PRESS

MATERIALS REQUIRED :

Old Books or flower press

Old belts

Flat, thin-leafed flowers

Water Colour Paper – Non-Bleached

Flower press   (optional)

WHAT TYPE OF FLOWERS:

Flowers that lay flat hold their color, and have thin petals are the best for pressing.

Gladiolus, Borage, Cosmos, Larkspur, Coreopsis, Queen Anne's Lace, Delphiniums, California poppies, Hibiscus, Geraniums (the individual flowers that make up the fluffy head), Verbenas, Nicotiana, and Pansies. Think single-ply leaves and flattened head.

You can test and flowers for pressing. Larger flowers like roses and dahlias will press, but they will become misshapen.

WHEN IS THE BEST TIME TO HARVEST FOR DRYING

Pick your flowers for pressing after the early morning dew has dried from the petals. You want your flowers fresh, but completely dry. Don't pick your flowers on a humid or rainy day.

BOOK METHOD FOR DRYING FLOWERS

Pressing flowers in old books is still a useful method for preserving flowers. It seems old-fashioned, but that's part of the charm.

It is best to use a large book, like a phone book (if you can find one) and either tie a strap or belt around it while pressing your flowers or add something substantial to the top to add pressure. You could also use old belts or straps to wrap around your book to tighten down the pages.

Print can sometimes rub off, or transfer, so it is a good idea to place your flowers between sheets of nonbleached paper before putting them inside of the book. Do this only if you want perfect natural dried flowers.

Another useful method uses a bleach-free hardbound watercolor notebook   . You will still need to add pressure to the top, but this is a pretty easy method that does not require adding additional pages.

Drying flowers this way takes about 30 days. If you open your book before the 30 days to peek, you risk cracking or breaking leaves. But after 30 days you will find your flowers beautifully pressed, and ready to use.

PRESS METHOD

You can buy or DIY a simple flower press using two pieces of wood with bolts in each corner. Stack the inside with pieces of cardboard, and double sheets of nonbleached paper.

To avoid transfers of print, use plain, unbleached, unprinted paper between your cardboard sheets.

You will want to give a tiny bit of space between each flower, don't overlap, but they can be placed relatively close together.

How to dry flowers with a press is simple but takes a bit of trial and error.

Pros for drying flowers with a press

Relatively cheap method.

Does not require special ingredients.

Easy to do, without any complicated instructions.

Creates beautiful flat flowers.

Pressed flowers make excellent craft project additions.

Cons for drying flowers with a press

Takes up to 30 days for perfect pressed flowers.

Flowers do not always retain their full vibrancy.

Flowers are delicate and can easily break.

HOW TO DRY FLOWERS – AIR DRY METHOD

WHAT TYPE OF FLOWERS

When air drying flowers you want to avoid flowers with lots of water content. They tend to not dry thoroughly and rot long before they ever dry out.

Flowers like African Marigolds, Cornflowers, Anise hyssop, Globe Thistle, Lady's Mantle, Hydrangeas, Larkspur, Lavender, Love in a mist, Dahlias (pompom), Poppy (Papaver types), Roses, Starflowers, Strawflowers, and Yarrow are good flowers to start with.

WHEN IS THE BEST TIME TO HARVEST FOR DRYING

In the morning, after the dew has dried and the flowers are their freshest. Pick blooms that are not fully open yet as they will open more as they dry out.

HOW TO AIR DRY FLOWERS

Start by gathering your flowers in bunches by the stem and secure them with a piece of string or rubber band. Hang them upside down in an area that receives good air flow. Make sure that your bunches are not too close together.

Hang the flowers in a cool dark place to dry out. Try to keep them out of the sunlight to retain some of their vivid colours.

Leave flowers for a few weeks to dry. You will notice the flowers will start to change colors. Bright, vibrant flowers change colour to browns, light pinks, dull yellows and transform into vintage bouquets. When the stems can snap easily, they are finished drying.

Use dried flowers in vases, or crafts like homemade wreaths, or even create centerpieces for the holidays.

Pros to air drying flowers

Minimum supplies required.

Easy for anyone to do.

Least expensive method.

Cons to air drying flowers

Very brittle petals.

Flowers lose much of their color and vibrancy.

Flowers shrink and crinkle.

This method is hit or miss, and you can lose flowers in the process. It is recommended to dry more than you think you will need because you will inevitably lose a few flowers along the way.

HOW TO DRY FLOWERS WITH SILICA GEL

MATERIALS NEEDED

Silica gel

Dust mask

Gloves

Airtight glass or plastic container

Flowers

Scissors or garden pruners

Plastic squeeze bottles

Mod Podge   or hairspray to seal flower from moisture

Optional: Microwave

**You can pick up silica sand / silica gel at most craft stores.

WHAT TYPE OF FLOWERS

Any! If they can fit in a container and if you have enough silica gel you should have no problem drying the largest of flowers.   Think roses, pansies, peonies, daisies, larkspur, carnations, bachelor buttons, zinnias, sunflowers, geraniums (worked but I did get a few batches of petals!), to name a few.

WHEN IS THE BEST TIME TO HARVEST FLOWERS FOR DRYING

Like other flowers, it is best to collect your flowers in the morning after the dew has dried and the flowers are freshest.   You will want fully opened blooms if you use the microwave method.

If you use the silica gel to dry your flowers without the microwave, pick flowers that are in full bloom.

SILICA GEL METHOD FOR DRYING FLOWERS

The flowers look like very realistic paper flowers, they even feel like paper.

Do not forget to put on your air filter mask and gloves before working with your silica gel.

Cut your flower stems about an inch away from your flower head.

Place your large flower heads face up in a container at least 2 inches taller than the flower. Flat faced flowers do better if you place them upside down. Flowers that are long, like larkspur, can be laid down on their sides.

Gently pour silica gel over the flowers until covered by an inch or more of silica gel. Place a lid on top, or saran wrap and set them aside for 3-5 days.

You need to be very gentle in removing your flowers, or you will end up with dried flower petals.

You can use a soft bristle paint brush to remove the remaining silica gel; it just dusts off.

USING THE MICROWAVE TO SPEED UP THE FLOWER DRYING PROCESS.

You can also use the microwave to dry your flowers. This method is fast and does a fantastic job of preserving vibrancy. If you are short on time, this is an excellent method for doing flowers quickly.

With two containers of silica gel, you can allow one batch to cool down while you work on the second one.

Use a microwave-safe container and cover your flowers entirely with about an inch of extra on the top. Pop in the microwave for a minute.

Let the container cool for 30 minutes before removing your dried flowers.

SEALING

You can seal your flowers with hairspray, mod podge, or with a rattle can spray varnish, be sure it is non-yellowing.

Pros of drying flowers with silica gel

Creates beautifully vibrant dried flowers.

Retains the same look like a freshly picked flower.

The fastest method by far, one minute in the microwave and your flowers are dry.

You can recharge silica gel by placing it in the oven for 30 minutes.

Cons of drying flowers with silica gel. Silica gel is one of the most expensive methods to start out with, but since the gel can be recharged the costs diminish over time.

Don't spill your silica gel because it is a pain to clean up!

You also need to use a filter mask and gloves while working with Silica gel.

You can make dried flower petals. Silica should be handled with gloves, and you have no sure way of knowing if you pulled all the silica from a dried flower.

DRYING FLOWERS IN A FOOD DEHYDRATOR

Food dehydrators work well for drying flowers. It's not as impressive as the silica gel, but it works.

MATERIALS NEEDED

Food dehydrator   (this is the one I use and it works great)

Flowers

Scissors or garden pruners

Mod Podge   or hairspray to seal flower from moisture

WHAT TYPE OF FLOWERS

You can dehydrate any small or medium-sized flower that will fit in your dehydrator. Small pom type flowers like zinnias, or marigolds do very well.

Larger flowers with delicate leaves like geraniums or tuberous begonias tend to take longer and end up a bit too brittle.

WHEN IS THE BEST TIME TO HARVEST FOR DRYING

Harvest your flowers at their full bloom early morning after the dew has dried.

DEHYDRATOR METHOD

Cut your flower stems close to the flowers. Place your flowers right side up but do not allow them to touch each other because they will stick.

For medium-sized flowers like pompom zinnias, or any cone style flowers, leave them for a few hours.

For small delicate flowers, like Queen Anne's lace, add for 1 hour but check on them periodically.

SEALING

You can seal your flowers with mod podge, hairspray, or a rattle can of spray sealer.

Pros for drying flowers with a food dehydrator

A relatively quick method, flowers can be dried in a few hours.

Easy process, no real fuss.

Perfect drying method if you want to make potpourri, or make dried petals.

Cons for drying flowers with a food dehydrator

You need a food dehydrator.

Some flowers, like French marigolds, leave a smell behind on your trays.

Overdrying can cause very brittle and delicate flowers.

Most flowers change color, especially the pinks purples and magentas that gained a deeper. ruddier color after drying. Yellow flowers generally held their color well.

DRYING FLOWERS WITH SAND OR KITTY LITTER

How to dry flowers with sand or kitty litter uses the same process as drying flowers with silica gel.

Drying with sand or kitty litter, it takes longer, and the results are a mixed bag. You can use it in a pinch and still get OK results

MATERIALS NEEDED

Sand or kitty litter

Airtight glass or plastic container

Flowers

Scissors or garden pruners

Mod Podge or hairspray to seal flower from moisture

WHAT TYPE OF FLOWERS

If your flowers can fit in a container and if you have enough sand or kitty litter you should have no problem drying most flowers.   Think roses, pansies, peonies, daisies, larkspur, carnations, bachelor buttons, or zinnias.   The larger, more delicate flowers like geraniums or peonies are hit and miss.

WHEN IS THE BEST TIME TO HARVEST FOR DRYING

Like all the other methods collect your flowers in the morning after the dew has dried and the flowers are freshest.

You will want partially opened blooms as the sand and kitty litter both take time to dry.

SAND, OR KITTY LITTER FLOWER DRYING METHOD

Cut your flower stems about an inch away from your flower head.

Place your large flower heads face up in a container at least 2 inches taller than the flower. Flat faced flowers do better if they are placed upside down. Flowers that are long, like larkspur, can be laid down on their sides.

Gently pour your kitty litter or sand over the flowers until covered by an inch. Place a lid on top, or saran wrap and set them aside for 10-21 days. (It's hit or miss here you will have to test and experiment)

You need to be very gentle in removing your flowers. The sand and kitty litter are heavy and can damage the shape of the flowers or weigh down and break off the petals. Go slow, pretend you're Indiana Jones without the fun and excitement.

You can use a soft bristle paint brush to remove the remaining sand or kitty litter.

Pros for drying flowers with sand or kitty litter

Inexpensive method.

Cons for drying flowers with sand or kitty litter.

The process is longer than say using silica gel.

Flowers can be easily damaged during removal.

Flowers do not keep or hold their vibrancy.

DIY Pressed Flower Easter Eggs

Here is what you will need:

White eggs, hard-boiled or empty

Pressed pansies or other pressed flowers

Wallpaper paste

A bowl

A small paintbrush

You can decorate hard-boiled or empty eggs. Use hard-boiled eggs when you want a sturdy egg for hiding and when you want to eat them when you're done (store them in the refrigerator). If you want to keep your eggs for a longer time and maybe even bring them out again next year, use empty eggs.

How to blow out eggs

Here is what you will need to blow out the eggs:

Needle or pin

Metal BBQ skewer

Wooden party skewer

Plastic food box

Tea towel

Instructions:

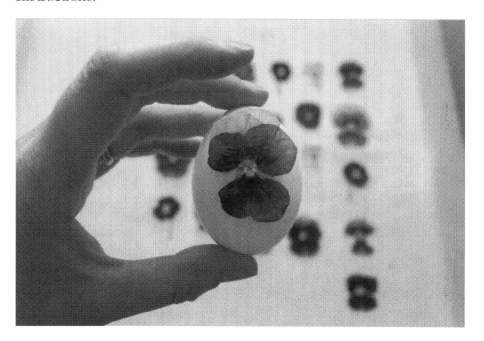

1. Make two tiny holes at either end of the egg using a needle or a pin.
2. The holes then need to be made bigger, so you can get the egg contents out. I used the metal BBQ skewer as a drill. Use your fingers to twist the skewer through the egg. Apply as little pressure as possible or the egg will crack.
3. Use the wooden party skewer to break up the yolk inside the egg, pushing it and out of the hole repeatedly.
4. Place the food box to catch the insides of the egg. Hold the egg right above the food box when you're blowing. If you use clean

materials, you can save the egg yolks and whites for scrambled eggs.

5. Blow hard into the hole with your mouth to get the egg to come out the other hole and into the box. If you are worried about salmonella poisoning and don't want to use your mouth, use a straw or an egg blowing tool.
6. Wash the hollowed-out eggs with water and soap. Blow out the water.
7. Put the eggs on a tea towel to dry overnight.

Pressed flower Easter eggs

1. Now that the eggs are empty and clean, it's time to decorate them.
2. Mix wallpaper paste and water in the bowl, make sure it is not too thick.
3. Apply the wallpaper paste on the back of the flowers with the brush.
4. Place the flower on the egg and use the paintbrush to gently smooth it onto the egg. Take a paper towel and carefully dab the leftover wallpaper paste. You can apply as many flowers to the egg as you like. I like to keep it simple.
5. Let them dry.

DIY Pressed Flower Iphone Case

You can make your own pressed flowers with a flower press or by placing them inside a large book, like an encyclopedia or phone book. If you are pressing your own flowers, keep in mind that the drying time takes a little while – usually a minimum of seven days.

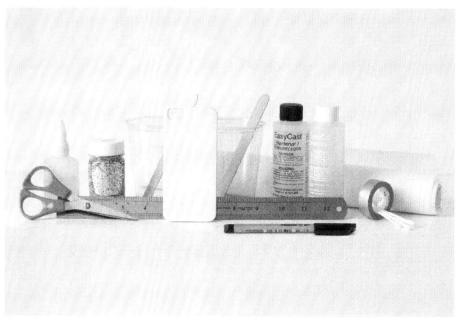

You will need:

Pressed dried flowers

Flat, solid white iPhone case

Clear craft glue

A flat and level work surface

Tape

Scissors

Parchment paper

Ruler

Thin-tip permanent marker

Timer

2 clear plastic cups

2 wooden craft sticks

50/50 clear-casting epoxy resin (I used Easy Cast)

Acetone (or a nail polish remover with acetone)

Q-tips

Glitter (Optional)

Intructions:

Step 1: Arrange the Flowers

To get started, place the pressed flowers on your case and play around with different flower arrangements. If you want to add a lot of flowers to your case, make sure that they don't pile up higher than 1/16th of an inch (approximately 1.5 mm) or you won't be able to properly coat the case in resin. Keep in mind that your pressed flowers will become slightly translucent once they are coated in resin,

31

so placing lighter colored flowers under darker ones works best. Once you have found an arrangement you like, take a snapshot of it for future reference.

Remove the flowers from the case and set them aside. Dab a small amount of glue on the largest flower and carefully glue it to the case. Follow suit with the rest of your flowers until your arrangement is complete.

Step 2: Prepare the Resin

Make sure you are in a well-ventilated area. Cut a 2 ft long (approximately 60 cm) piece of parchment paper with your scissors and tape it down to your flat work surface. Take your resin and read the directions carefully. (Note: If the directions for your resin differ from the steps below, make sure to follow the directions for your resin or you'll end up with a sticky mess, and that's no good for placing a flowery phone call!)

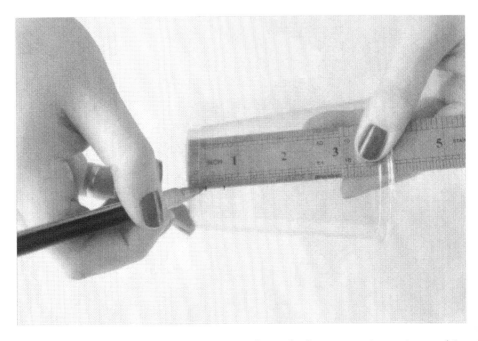

Put your ruler inside a plastic cup and mark the cup twice using a thin permanent marker. Your first mark will be at 3/8 of an inch, and your second will be at 3/4 of an inch.

Set your timer to 2 minutes and have a craft stick ready for stirring. Slowly pour resin into the cup up to the 3 /8 inch line. Keep in mind that an accurate pour is crucial, so don't be too generous with your pour. Next, slowly pour the hardener to the 3/4 inch line, making sure to not go over it.

Start the timer and stir the contents of the cup with your craft stick for 2 minutes, making sure to scrape the sides of the cup from time to time. Don't worry if you see lots of bubbles forming in the cup – they'll disappear later. When the timer goes off, place the second plastic cup on your work surface and have your second unused craft stick ready for stirring. Optional: If you would like to add glitter to your case, sprinkle some into the mix now.

Next, set your timer to 1 minute and pour the contents of the first cup into the second cup. Continue stirring until the timer goes off. Let the resin rest for 5 minutes.

Step 3: Add Resin to the Case

Slowly pour a small amount of your newly mixed resin onto the center of your case. It's always better to err on the side of caution and add too little resin than too much.

Spread the resin close to the edge of your case using your craft stick. Make sure the resin does not go over the edge. Add more resin to the case until the entire back and all the flowers are covered. Lightly blow on any bubbles that show up on the surface to help them disappear.

Set the case down on the parchment paper and keep an eye on it as it dries (about one to two hours). If any resin spills over the edges, dip Q-tips in acetone and wipe clean.

Once your first coat of resin has dried, examine your case to make sure all the flowers have been properly coated. If needed, add a second coat of resin.

Voila! You now have an embellished floral phone case to brighten up any conversation.

DIY Dried Flower Pendant

You will need:

Judikins Diamond Glaze

E6000 Multi-Purpose Adhesive

25mm Pendant Blanks with Glass Cabochons (I bought mine on Etsy from LagunaCraftSupply. The cost was $20 for 20 blanks which included the glass cabochons.)

Organza necklaces (I got mine from CandyTiles2. Cost was $3.95 for 10.)

Jump rings (I used 4.5 mm 16g heavy duty sterling silver jump rings from Etsy seller RaineSupplies. Silver plated would be a more economical option.)

dried flowers (I used Queen Anne's Lace, which worked well. Be careful using flowers that have delicate petals such as pansies etc. You would need to coat the delicate petals in Mod Podge before gluing the cabochon.)

tweezers

cardstock (try to avoid card stock that has a porous surface, as the glue will soak into it creating blotches.)

Round Nose Micro Pliers

Jewelers Flat Nose Plier

Lay out your wildflower.

If using Queen Anne's Lace, snip off a piece of the flower that will fit beneath the cabochon and use tweezers to place it on your piece of card stock. Adhere the flower use a wee bit of e-6000. (I applied the glue sparingly with a toothpick.)

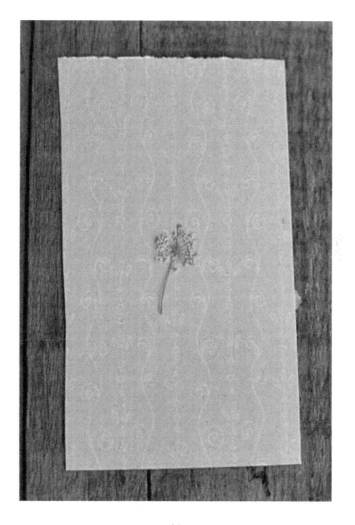

Position your glass cabochon over the flower.dried flower pendant

Place three drops of diamond glaze on the back of your glass cabochon. Try to stay in the middle of the glass.

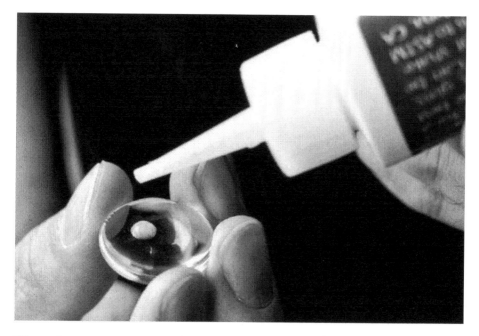

Place the cabochon over the flower and hold in place for 45 seconds pressing hard.

Let dry for ten minutes, then cut around glass cabochon.

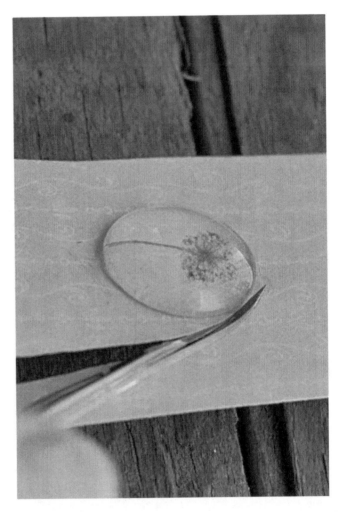

Add e-6000 glue to back of cabochon using a toothpick. Spread evenly. Don't use too much! Press cabochon inside pendant blank. Hold until set. Let dry for 15 minutes. Add jump ring.

Add organza necklace. You're done!

DIY Pressed Wildflower Bookmark

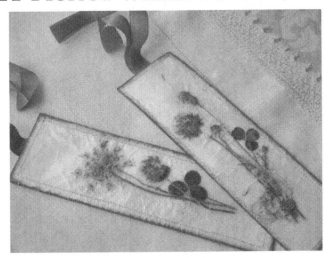

You will need:

3 ply tissue

Aleene's tacky glue

Reynolds wax paper

Bits of fiber

Ink

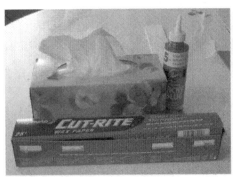
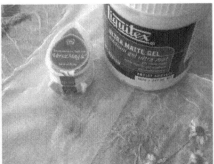

So let's get started. Combine a mixture of approx' 60% glue to 40% water. You don't want it too watery and you don't want it too gluey either.

Mix it really well with an old brush.

You can add some fiber at this point too so it is under the glue mixture, or add it later with gel medium.

Grab a tissue from the box and separate it into 3 ply's, you are only going to use 1 ply. Make sure you are not in a breezy room to do this, or have a fan blowing.

Take your tissue and gently place over your arrangement. Dab it gently and not too much, don't over do it or the tissue with split open on you.

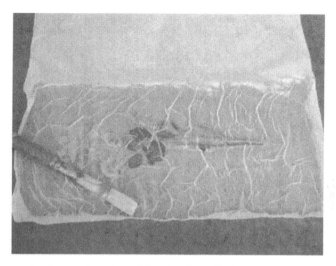

ow you have to be patient and let it dry all day or overnight. Then it will look like this ....

Next step: If you are making a bookmark, cut out two pieces of white "watercolor paper" in the size you would like your bookmark.

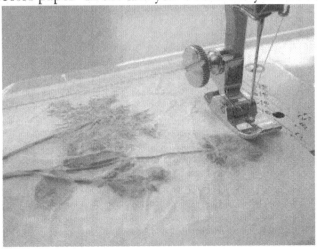

Tidy up your threads and bring it back to your glue table.

Turn over the piece you have stitched on and place some ribbon as shown below. Glue this to the paper and then glue your second piece of watercolor paper over top of this.

Another option is to punch a hole in the bookmark when it is finished, then add ribbon.

When that has dried which isn't long, turn it over the front again.

Now you can edge the front with the green ink too.

Don't forget these are just my steps, you can do whatever your little heart desires, use any ink, any thread etc etc, just do your thing

If you didn't add any fibers under the tissue, you can still do it now. Take a very teeny tiny amount and lay it where you like the look of it. Make sure to let it dry well.

Now you have a pretty bookmark, which would make a lovely gift with a book or for a garden/nature lover, for anyone really, wouldn't you love one?

Printed in Great Britain
by Amazon

35787161R00031